ROZANNE *TRACKS* POLAR BEARS
AT EDGE OF ARCTIC

(Book 2 of *Rozanne's Wildlife Travels* Series)

BY ROZANNE WEISSMAN

Bethesda Communications Group

Published by
Bethesda Communications Group
49 Wellesley Circle
Glen Echo, MD 20812
www.bcgpub.com

ISBN-13: 978-1-7367773-9-8
ISBN-10: 1-7367773-9-4

DEDICATION

Dedicated to the world's children who LOVE wildlife
To my special children's book consultants Rose & Nora
To those who helped me regain strength since pandemic losses:
Kendal Black, CORE PT
Personal Trainers Diane Allan and Dave Williams

PHOTOGRAPHY CREDITS

Author Rozanne Weissman took most
photos on an iPhone 14 Pro and created
the entire book on an iPhone.

Photo credits to Natural Habitat Adventures (NHA)
Expedition Leader Lianne Thompson who shot
with a telephoto lens ALL the three (3) bears shots
and some others. Other fellow travelers and
expedition leaders, including those who moderate
NHA Daily Doses of Nature.

Photos also from Daniel Raiti Photography.
TINY photo of polar bears swimming underwater
from Picture of His Life documentary
by wildlife photographer Amos Nachoum.
Back cover photo from Shutterstock.

PROLOGUE
(WHAT HAPPENED BEFORE)

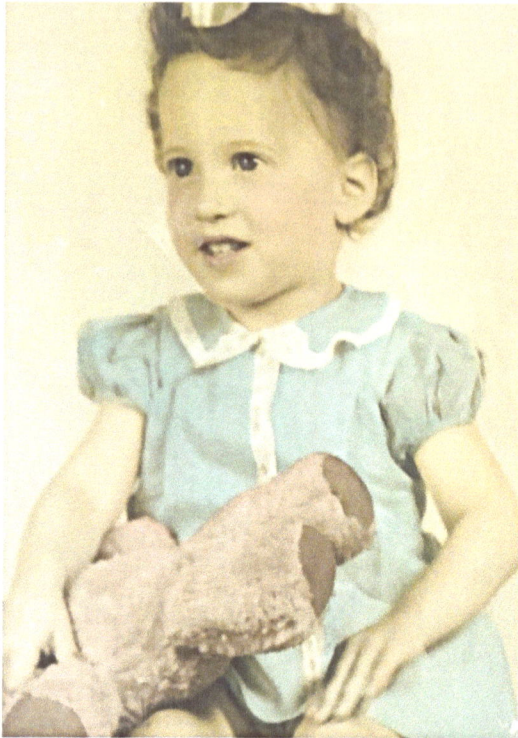

When Rozanne grows up, she didn't want to just watch wild animals on TV 📺 and movies 🎥. She wants to travel to where wildlife lives—in the wild.

AUTHOR
Rozanne Weissman

When Rozanne was a child, she LOVED ❤️ her stuffed teddy bear and wild animals. *Do you?* She remembers watching a caterpillar 🐛 magically turn into a butterfly 🦋.

The full leopard
RozanneWeissman.com

Rozanne Weissman's first children's book,
Rozanne Travels to Africa to Kiss 💋 a Giraffe,
shares her 3 AMAZING wildlife journeys.

AUTHOR ROZANNE:

🐾 "SITS WITH" red-haired orangutans in
rainforests of Borneo, Indonesia!

🐾 SEES 5 elusive (hard to find) leopards, including 2 leopard cubs!
Rozanne is the ONLY person to see 5! High 5 ✋ Rozanne!

🐾 ADOPTS a baby orphaned elephant and
KISSES 💋 a giraffe in Kenya, Africa.

Rozanne's Wildlife Travels YouTube channel
"TRANSPORTS" children with her on her travels!

ROZANNE'S FOURTH WILDLIFE JOURNEY

Where does Rozanne travel on her fourth wildlife journey? To REMOTE Churchill, Canada, the "Polar Bear Capital of the World."

Polar bears gather near the Hudson Bay until ice forms. Churchill is on the edge of the Arctic ("subarctic").

Population: 800 humans, 750 polar bears!

The nearest city is 1000 miles away.
There are NO roads.

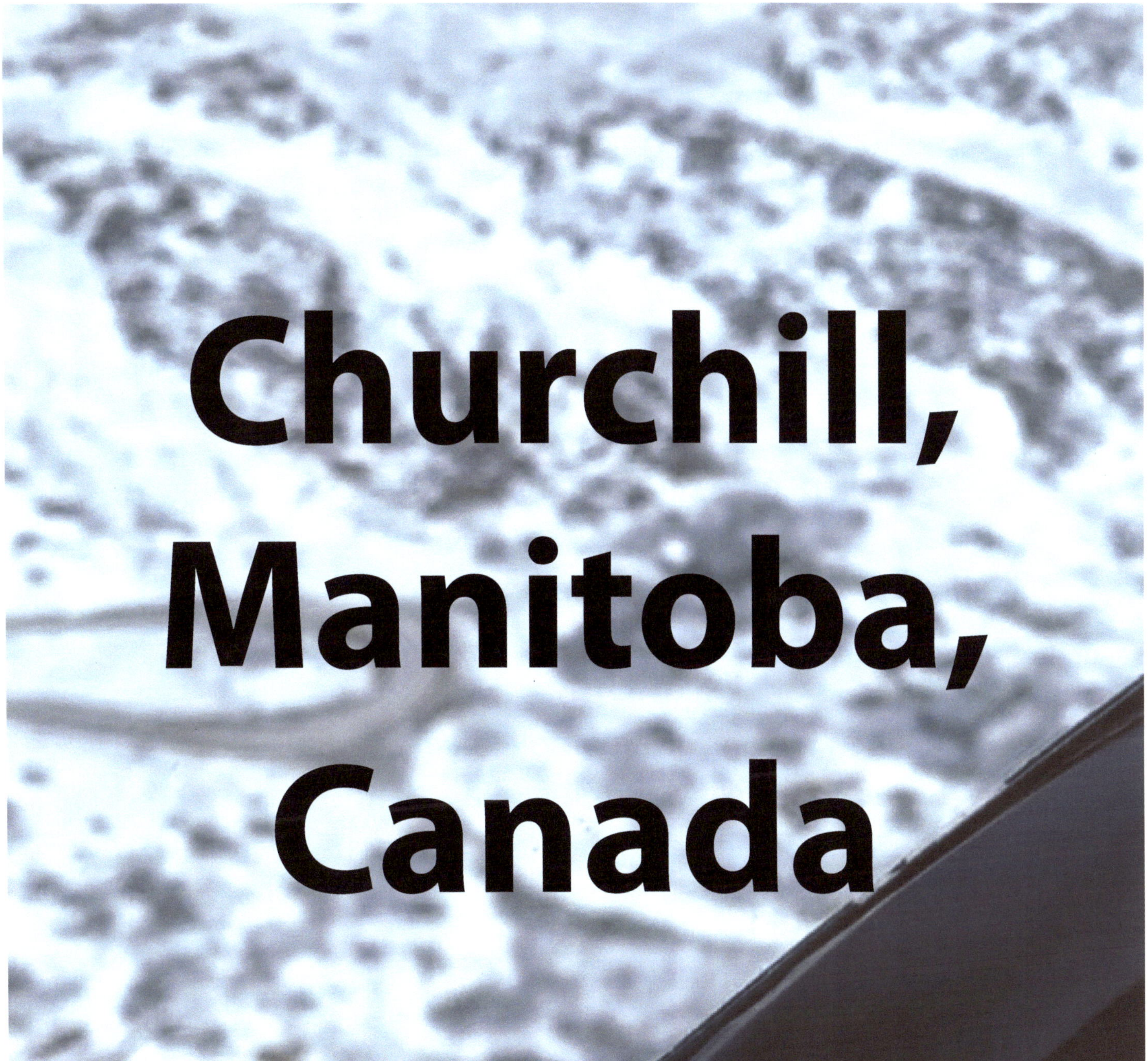
Churchill,
Manitoba,
Canada

(Aerial view)

Polar bears are FIERCE.
Polar bear warning signs are EVERYWHERE.

Homes and cars are UNLOCKED so that
people can ESCAPE polar bears!

Yet, all Rozanne sees in town
where people live and work:

🐾 Fierce-looking stuffed polar bear in a museum
🐾 Polar bear pooping art in a bathroom
🐾 Polar bear pillows in her room

POLAR BEAR

NO REAL
POLAR BEARS
HERE!

Be Bear Aware

LOOK BEFORE
EXITING BUILDING

Five (5) nations with the most polar bears signed a historic treaty in Oslo, Norway, to protect polar bears. The date: November 15, 1973. Before that, many polar bears were hunted or shot in towns.

To mark the 50th anniversary of the treaty, Rozanne timed the release of her wildlife children's book on polar bears for November 2023.

Dangerous polar bears that are found near town with people are lured into traps…

Then they go to "polar bear jail." All they get is water to discourage them from returning, keeping both people and polar bears SAFE.

Rozanne in orange scarf 🧣
stands in front of polar bear jail.

DOG
SLED
PARKING
←→
VIOLATORS
WILL BE
PEED ON

DOGSLEDDING

Rozanne is excited to go dogsledding!

In his cabin, Dave Daley explains what each dog does on a dogsled.

Travel company owner
Dave Daley loves 🧡 his sled dogs.
Do YOU have a dog you LOVE?

He raised Rea since she was little
with a broken leg.

Now, they "sing" 🎶 and sled together.

Dave's hard-working Northern Husky sled dogs
look at Dave as "Big Dog" or "boss."

*White Northern Husky Rea in lower left photo
sings with "Big Dog Dave" here and also on
Rozanne's Wildlife Travels YouTube channel.*

14

Rozanne is so excited.
She is going on her first dogsled ride!

The dogs are LOUDLY

BARKING

BARKING

BARKING

in excitement!

Rozanne in the purple pants
rushes to the first dogsled.
Did the dog turn around to look at Rozanne?
Silly Rozanne.

The dog looks to "Big Dog Dave" for instructions.

The dog team races through the "boreal forest"—
northernmost forests, with what Rozanne calls
"skinny trees," with needles, no leaves
—like pine, fir, spruce.

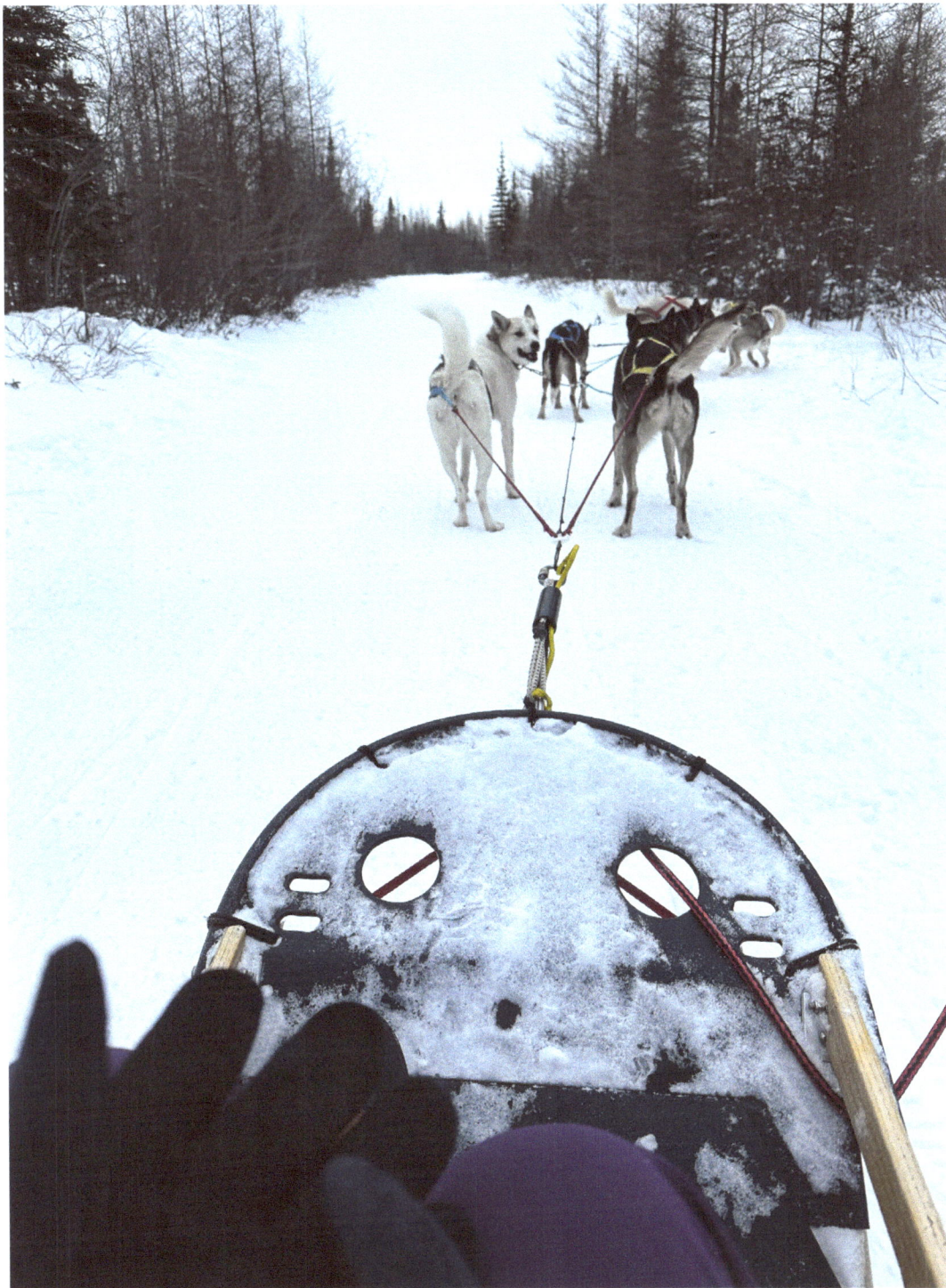

As a joke, the sled ride is named "Ididamile"
(I Did a Mile!) after the famous
Alaska 1,000 mile dogsled race
"Iditarod" ("distant place").

Rozanne in the orange scarf
wants MORE!

Rozanne sees NO POLAR BEARS ANYWHERE!

HELICOPTER TO POLAR BEAR DEN

Rozanne goes on a helicopter 🚁 ride
to a polar bear den!

How cool 😎 is that?

From the helicopter, she sees
moose. *How many moose do you see*?

The helicopter 🚁 lands.
It is snowing and deep
walking

down

down

down

down

to the EMPTY polar bear den.

A tour leader in a red jacket 🧥
slides down into the den.
Rozanne would be scared. *Would you be?*
She comes out with the "all OK" sign.

Rozanne sees NO POLAR BEARS ANYWHERE!

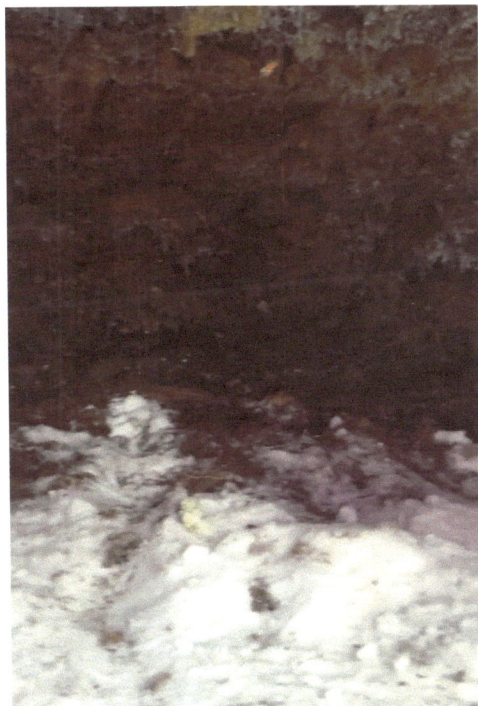

SURPRISING POLAR BEAR FACTS

* *What color skin do polar bears have?* It's actually black to match the nose! The 2 layers of fur that "appear white" are actually clear!

* Polar bear cubs are born with a pink tongue 👅 that turns blue, purple, or black.

* A male polar bear can weigh as much as 10 men!

* Polar bears have feet the size of dinner plates! Hairy soles insulate their feet and prevent slipping.

* Polar bears can SMELL their favorite "prey" (animal food like ringed seals) more than half a mile away—even under ice!

* Pregnant polar bears dig a den in fall where they give birth, care for their cubs, and emerge in springtime.

* Mama polar bears can go 4-8 months without food. They care for and teach cubs for 2 1/2 years.

• *Do polar bears and penguins 🐧 live in same freezing 🥶 areas?* Penguins & polar bears would NEVER be together in the wild! Polar bears 🐼 live in Arctic & subarctic countries. Penguins live in Antarctica. See BOTH on *Rozanne's Wildlife Travels* YouTube channel.

• Polar bears are the ONLY bears classified as marine (water) mammals. They spend most time on sea ice AND can swim for days.

• Biggest threat to polar bears: Long-term climate trend of warmer temperatures. Sea ice forms later and melts earlier.

WHY SHOULD HUMANS CARE?

Arctic sea ice 🥶 is important for humans. It reflects sunlight and keeps worldwide temperatures down . It's the earth's "air conditioner."

Rozanne gets into the large polar Rover to
FINALLY TRACK 🐾 polar bears.

The vehicle is HUGE!

TALL wheels lift it so the polar bears can't get onto
the outdoor deck where wind-blown Rozanne is.

Rozanne did not see any polar bears YET.

But she did see her first Arctic fox and Arctic hare!

Rozanne with
orange scarf 🧣
TRACKS SO MANY
polar bears!

**THEY HAD NOT
EATEN FOR 145
DAYS—NO SEA
ICE as the climate
warms!!!**

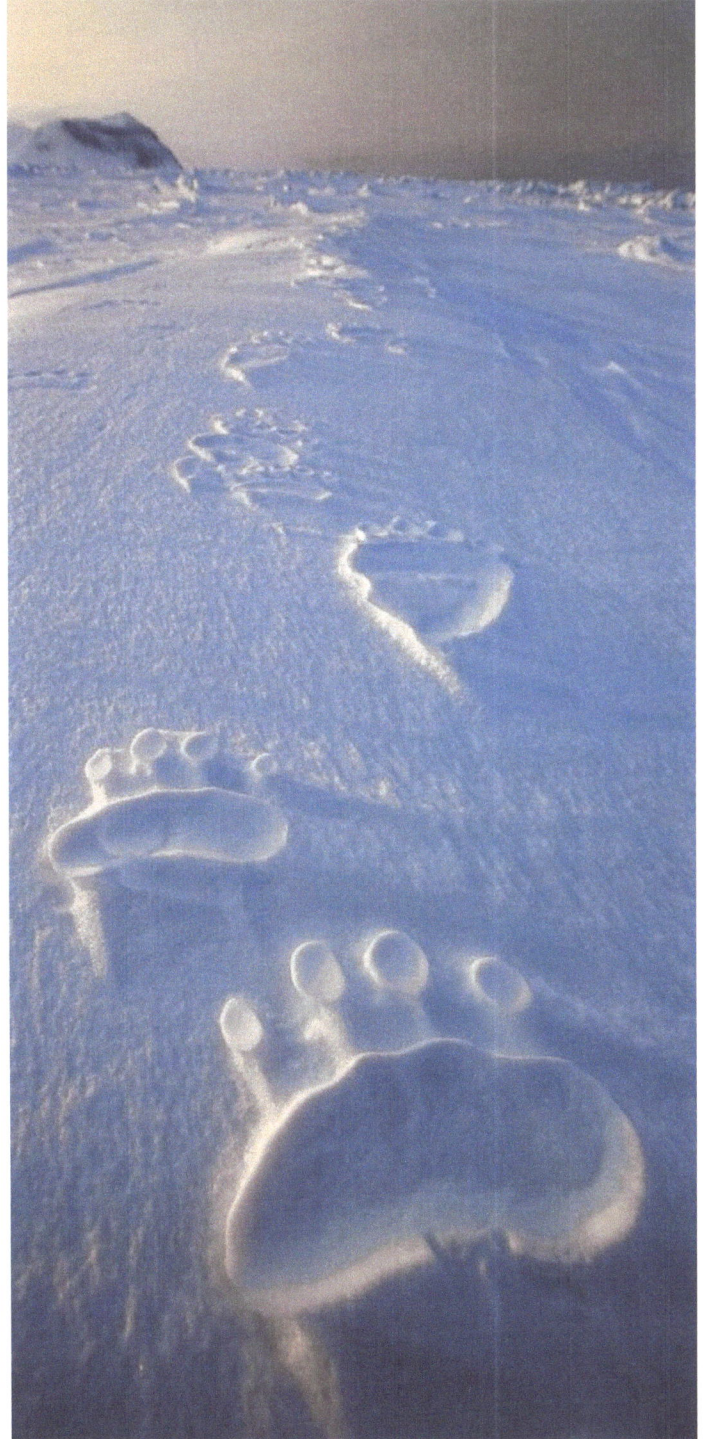

WHY POLAR BEARS NEED SEA ICE!

Then the Rover drives closer to the Hudson Bay
where polar bears gather
to wait for ice to form.

It is early November, and they are testing the ice to
see if it holds them—jumping and spreading
out their whole body with butt up!

Polar bears need sea ice to live,
mate, hunt, travel, and rest.
They TRAVEL LONG DISTANCES
on sea ice.

It's their PLATFORM TO HUNT AND GRAB UPWARD
onto the sea ice their favorite food:
fatty ringed seals.

Testing the ice

THREE (3) BEARS

Rozanne's Natural Habitat Adventures
tour leader Lianne Thompson spots 3 bears
sleeping through her binoculars.

Rozanne recalls the story of
"Three (3) Little Bears" from her childhood.

We wait in the warm Rover to see
what they might do when they wake up.

3 bears sleeping. Then they start to awaken and get up.

Polar bears playing. And polar bear sniffing.

2 bears size each other up as 1 bear watches.
Then they tumble around.

2 polar bears sparring. This is mostly play fighting to get them ready for real fights. Males fight during mating season over females.

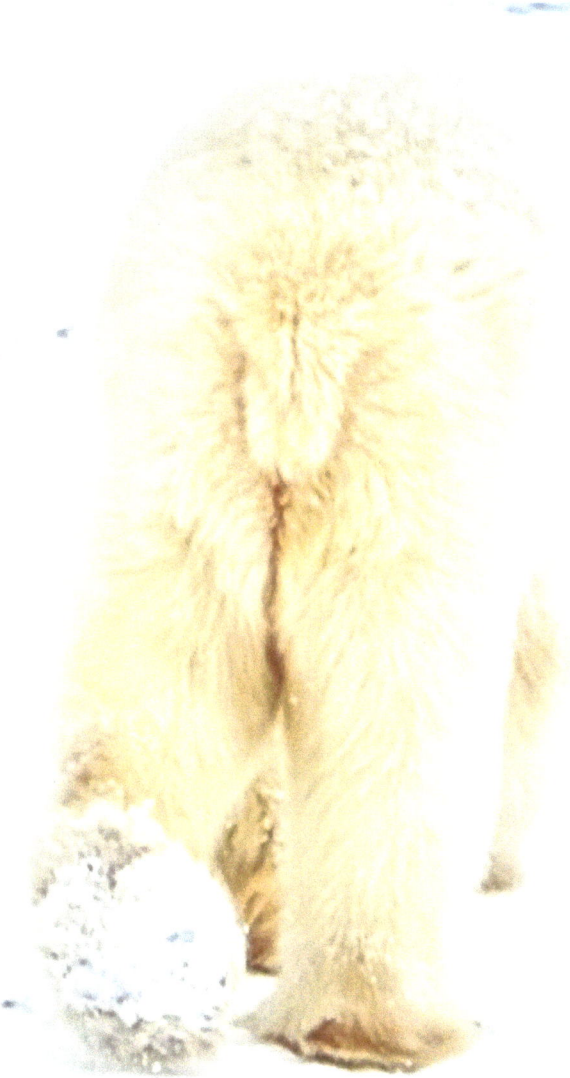

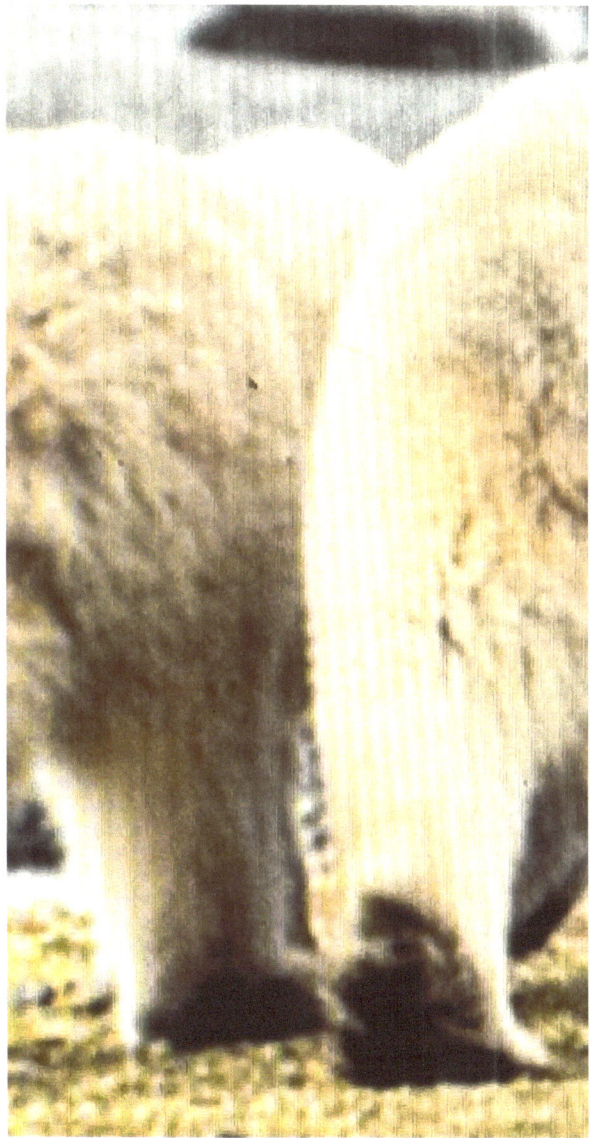

THE END

ABOUT THE AUTHOR

Wildlife Children's Book Author Rozanne Weissman debuted her second timely new book, *Rozanne Tracks⁕ Polar Bears at Edge of Arctic,* in November 2023.

The author timed the release of her new book to honor the 50th anniversary of the signing of a major treaty to protect polar bears. The treaty was signed by five nations with the most polar bears in Oslo, Norway, November 15, 1973.

Before that, polar bears were routinely trophy-hunted and shot if near towns and people. Now polar bears face another big issue: Loss of sea ice "home" in a warming climate.

Rozanne's three previous wildlife journeys are covered in her first highly acclaimed children's book, *Rozanne Travels to Africa to Kiss a Giraffe*—30+ 5-star reviews on Amazon. Pre-pandemic, the book was extensively tested with children, teachers, and heads of schools. Drafts changed with input.

Rozanne's books are unique in the children's book genre:
- REAL stories vs fantasy
- REAL photos vs illustrations
- Emojis—children want more
- *Rozanne's Wildlife Travels* YouTube channel accompanies books
- School classroom live and virtual visits
- Children book consultants
- Inspiration for disabled

Despite Disabilities
Rozanne's books represent an unimaginable, new career. She was asked to create the the first book of her wildlife travels with her photos "for the children" at a school where she volunteered.

With hand/wrist disabilities and NO COMPUTER (doctor's orders), Rozanne created BOTH books on an iPhone—dictating on Siri and laying out photos and content on an app.

Previous Career
Prior to this, Rozanne was a renowned Washington, DC- based marketing/communications exec and consultant with 60 national and international awards.

***Rozanne's Wildlife Travels* YouTube channel**
https://youtube.com/@RozannesWildlifeTravels

RozanneWeissman.com

www.ingramcontent.com/pod-product-compliance
Lightning Source LLC
Chambersburg PA
CBHW061357090426
42739CB00003B/46